MW01098223

I Forgot My Parachute This Time

I Forgot My Parachute This Time

A Collection of Poetry in Three Acts

by Jordan Broberg

Columbus, Ohio

I Forgot My Parachute This Time: A Collection of Poetry in Three Acts

Published by Gatekeeper Press
2167 Stringtown Rd, Suite 109
Columbus, OH 43123-2989
www.GatekeeperPress.com

The cover design is the product of Zach Blumner and the editorial work for the cover is the product of Sarah Schecker. Gatekeeper Press did not participate in and is not responsible for any aspect of these elements.

Library of Congress Control Number: 2021934993

ISBN (hardcover): 9781662911576

Table of Contents

Act 1

The Opening

SEVEN GRAND PT. I

I remember pulling my hair up into a bun
because things were getting serious between us.
I needed to see you clearly
before I kicked your ass
at billiards.
This all began with a game.
It usually does.
I'm still not sure
who's the cat
and who's the mouse.
But from that moment
over green felt and cue sticks,
over the smell of burnt whiskey
and your warm cologne,
I decided I wanted
you.
At this bar.
In this town.
We both enjoyed the challenge
but fuck —
looks like I was outta luck
because right corner pocket,
I hit that eight ball in.
Clean.

Was that foreshadowing?
Hope this is worth allowing.

TABLE READ

Your eyes meet mine across the table.
Suddenly the play isn't what we're reading anymore.

THE TELEPHONE

Electric currents
through our lines
between you and I.

Minutes to the hour,
hours to the day,
you have me in every way.

Talking about nothing
and everything
in the same vine.

You can always
call me to kill
the time.

MY GREATEST CONTRADICTION

I'm leaving for my dreams.
October's coming fast.
The leaves that I'll soon see
will change colors.
I'll taste the bitter cold
and get screamed at by strangers.
The streets will be busy with
marquees glistening on every corner.
My body will have a greater sense of purpose.
I cannot wait.
But if you say what I want you to say,
damn —
I just might.
I just might stay.

And I hate that
with every fiber
in my bloodlust of a being
because I can't do that for you.
But, just ask?
Make me stay.
Okay.
I'm begging you.
Persistence is the key and
I'll come around.
I swear.
You have to trust me.
It really won't be that hard.
I promise.

Keep telling me that where I'm going
has shitty weather.
Or that it doesn't have the same views
and parks and suns as the city of angels does.
Or that it doesn't have the same magic.
Or that we can't go to our arcade anymore.
Or that we can't ride with your top down on the freeway anymore.
Or that we can't look at each other and not say what we're too afraid to say anymore.

Convince me to stay,
then please
let me go.

INTIMACY NO. 5

This time you saw
my pale frame in morning light.
I'm sure it blinded your eyes
but you didn't care
and neither did I.
You wanted to see me
uncovered,
unhidden,
unapologetic.
The newness was startling.
I was used to feeling in the dark,
like somehow I needed more air
but my lungs couldn't expand.
This time,
I saw your eyes
when they caught the sun.
And my lungs opened.

I never thought
in this kind of intimacy
I'd find myself in a goldmine.

PULLING TEETH

Something has cracked.
I feel it through your back
as you lie in the opposite direction.

Mountains are separating us in this bed.
Mountains you've built.
Can you feel it?

"I'm just tired."
We're all fucking tired
but I'm not your dentist
and I won't beg for the
movement of your jaw
just to make me feel better.

You are letting these mountains grow.
So don't be surprised
when you try to reach for me
and you're up in the sky all alone.

SCOOTER

In the middle of the night
passing blurred marquee lights,
there's you and I.

You're behind me,
arms at your side,
looking up at the sky,
riding your bike.

I zoom ahead on my scooter.
When I turn to see your face
I fall while flying through the street.

The scooter suffered no damage.

MOP

This game is exhilarating and exhausting.
Perhaps it's exactly how we've lasted.
'Cause you haven't left just yet.
Neither have I.

How sustainable is this?
I want words.
Any words from your mouth.
I'm not asking for much.
Am I?
I don't mean to
but words mean something.
You should know this.
You're a writer,
right?

Do you feel anything when you read this?
You must.
We're full of feelings.
We just don't articulate them with our tongues.
So we'll articulate in other ways
where we can hide
behind the pleasures of
our skin
and our pride.

I warn you though.
Pride will be our downfall
and our lack of words
will make us
empty.

But I'm ready to be filled.

Fill me to the very brim.
I'm not scared to tip over.
I'm not scared to spill everything I am
onto the floor.
I can always mop it up
and leave no residue.

THE DANGER OF ASSOCIATING YOU WITH ROCK 'N' ROLL

As a baby my mother would play it for me
so I could fall asleep.
When she turned the radio off,
I burst into a flood of tears.

From then on
I slept with the radio every single night.
And although my ma needed her rest,
she couldn't bear hearing me
cry until the sky changed colors.

And this was the first thing I realized
I couldn't live without.

DECK OF CARDS

I'm scrambling now to get it all down.
I should have started writing for you a long time ago.
I don't want to forget the things you've said to me and
my little fingers can only move so fast,
but they always try their best.

I begin catapulting your words to the page.
My mind races back to one of our very first conversations.
You were hunched over a piano.
My body was halfway out of the classroom door.

"You play your cards very close to your chest."

Three years ago
and you already knew
my greatest weakness.
Perhaps it's my greatest strength.
But by the end of this,
all of my cards will be on the table
and I'm not gonna fold.

I've never known how.

WHIPLASH

The journey has been
unpredictable, electric
and thrilling
beyond measure.
But the space between joy
and the jolt of heartbreak
occurs too quickly.
I'm afraid it will snap.
I guess some part of myself has accepted
that a broken neck is worth it
if it's your foot on the gas.

YOU WILL, TOO

I don't need you to take care of me.
I wouldn't dream of it.
But I might wear your t-shirts
and use your shower and ask you
to pick me up at the train station.
I don't need you to call me beautiful.
That isn't necessary when I feel it every time you look at me.
But I might call you beautiful and hold your hands and
hope that's enough.
I don't need you to change.
I would never ask you to.
But I might call your bluff and push your potential
and demand you know that
you are worth the world.
I don't need you to be mine.
I couldn't put you in a box.
But I might want to and that scares me.
And I know that would scare you.

Because I would be so good to you.
So good for you.
No jealousy,
no calamity.
No pressure,
just presence.
It's been three summers now.
You still may not see it.
Maybe you'll come around
or maybe you won't.
I'll be okay.
You will, too.

DEATH OF PROXIMITY / SHE

It's the last night of me living in this city.
Convenience has come to an end.
I fear this is it.
Let's call it quits.
Let's?

You'll have another shortly
who messes up your sheets,
who uses your shaving cream,
who drinks all your amaretto,
who lets you grip her body like a python,
who is better at lying,
better at fucking,
better at making you feel
like there isn't a gaping hole in your chest.
She will be all of those things for you
and more.
We don't own each other.
We don't owe each other a thing.

I CAN SEE YOUR RIBCAGE

I'm too open, too weak.
Too bold, yet too meek.
Honesty's the bastard child of courage and fear.
God it's been three fucking years.
What are you waiting for?
I've been holding myself so long I'm sore.
I'd rather not just sit here and seethe.
I need something, even through gritted teeth.
But cowards are comfortable,
they'll never get what they need.
They only know how to starve
because they are too scared to feed.

WHEN THE LAUGHTER BECOMES THE MUSIC

The sun hits my legs through your blinds, but I'm already awake.
Awake because I want you.
And I couldn't catch a wink of sleep because of it.
So I blame my boundless lust on your horrendous snoring instead.
I don't watch you when you sleep though.
Not now.
It feels like an invasion of privacy.
You've let me into your home,
so the least I can do is let you dream in peace
or in pieces.
But something shifts.
Your hand fits perfectly into my hip
and I know you're awake too.
Your eyes open.
I come undone.
You've undone me with one look.
All parts of me.
But no.
You would rather make me laugh until everything hurts.
You go for your bluetooth speaker.

"This will be our sex playlist. Only this song.
On repeat. The entire time."

"Part of Your World" from Disney's, *The Little Mermaid*.
Of course.
We chuckle through our kisses.
"Wandering free,
wish I could be…"

This is the moment.
This is the moment where I realize
my favorite thing to taste
is your laughter.

THE GARDENER

My fascination for you is endless.
I am enraptured by you.
When we spend the day together,
something is planted.
I exit through your door much differently
than how I entered.
And I feel like maybe, just maybe,
I'm beginning to know
you.
This is why I must go.
I can't have you all figured out.
I'll get bored
if I'm too close.
I'll abandon you
or you'll abandon me.
That is the last thing I want.
I was here to help plant the garden,
but I must leave in order for it to grow.

DILATION, REVELATION

You leaned into me.
My back pressed up against
your kitchen chair.
The room was dark
and my two grays widened.
You caught me.
No chance to brace myself.
No chance to prepare.
It was written all over my face
and there was nothing I could do.

SLAUGHTER ALL SENTIMENT

There is no other option.
I'm leaving,
you have no feelings,
and that's that.
Let's pretend
just for a moment,
that you do.
If the scenario played out
the exact way I wanted,
you still wouldn't show it
which is complete and utter
bullshit.
I can't even say how I feel
so I spend time smashing computer keys
to find something real.
What if you run away.
"No expectations" is all you'll say.
So I'll do the running for us.
Don't worry.
I'll run east to the city
where another beauty will find me.

Kill before it kills you.
Because we don't have another choice,
do we?

GHOST ON THE DANCE FLOOR

I'm slipping
out of your sheets,
into the street
with no sleep,
and leaving.
I felt sick.
I feel sick.
I wasn't lying,
I swear.
Last night was the first time you didn't see me.
You saw through me.
I extended my hand,
to which you denied
and it cut like a knife
through the rainbows and disco light,
through the pulsating rhythm of night,
your eyes met someone else.
You invited her in for a long time.
You didn't let her leave.
You gawked at her body
and undressed her with your eyes.
I felt my body rage.
I wanted to go astray
but you took me home
and undressed me anyway.
I feel so small.
Significantly insignificant,
that's me.
But not jealousy,
that vice will never get the best of me.

All I can do is thank you
for the reminder that you are not mine.
Do yourself a favor,
take her off that dance floor next time
and take her home.
I'm gonna dance anyway,
even if it means dancing alone.

SEVEN GRAND PT. II

Same bar.
Same town.
Same jukebox.
Same round.
But a different You sits across from me.
Different from the You two summers ago,
where this began with a game of pool
and a little courage,
but not the liquid kind.
I didn't need it back then.
I need it now.
I have a drink this time.

Now there's a different Me sitting across from you too.
Our bar,
our town.

I like this.
Perhaps too much.
I might say or do
something incredibly stupid.
Yet this is the first time
I have a viable excuse.

ANTICIPATION

My favorite space between us
is not in-between the sheets
or in-between our words.

It's the space in-between our faces
where I watch you make the decision
to kiss me.

Because in that space,
we are in-between who we are
and who we could be.

CROP CIRCLES

Stay rational,
stay rational.
Keep it clasped
in all the ways you can fit.

Don't let it in,
don't let it in.
The sin sinks deeper,
you thought you outran it.

Skin and bones,
skin and bones.
Just looking for a home,
thought it could be you.

Burnt and shredded,
burnt and shredded.
You left with no explanation,
this I already knew.

(MI.) TO NEW YORK CITY 1

The distance
that will become habitual
is defined by your name.
Maybe I'm just running away
from things too harrowing to say,
but running is still moving forward.
I will find my sense of direction.

But how can I be
separated by two thousand,
seven hundred
and eighty-nine
of you?

I've never been apart from you.
I'll always be a part of you.

IF MY BODY WAS A HOUSE, MY HEART WOULD BE THE DOOR

It's the constant cycle
of being open and closed
and my hinges are far beyond repair.
They broke long ago.
You broke them.
You kept swinging me open
and slamming me shut
over
and over
and over.
They were once in mint condition
'cause you can't break hinges on a door
that nobody ever
took the time
or the patience
or the curiosity
to even turn the knob.
Yet you came along
with a crowbar
and you badgered me
and you questioned me
and forced me not to lie
about my feelings
and eventually
my wood started to split open
and tarnish
and crack
and everything that I was
had splintered off into pieces
and I couldn't keep it together for you
anymore.

DAGGERS

You said that about my eyes.
They're silver, like the blades of knives.
I'm sure I've sent you looks
that have cut you open wide.
You asked me what I see in your eyes
and the most vibrant color so far is pride.
But I do see someone looking for themselves,
someone who doesn't want to hide.
So when I say I see myself in them,
know I'm not telling you a lie.
Daggers might be deadly weapons,
but if used correctly
they could save your life.

SORRY FOR BEING MORBID

If you saw my name on the TV as a casualty,
whether it be in a car, in a church,
a hotel, a grocery store,
a festival, a park,
a theater you've been to with me before,
would you wish
you would have said
the things you were
too afraid to say?
What if you saw a bullet
go through my chest
or some drunken jackass
pulls a hit-and-run
and you try your best
to avoid them but you can't
and before you know it,
I'm at permanent rest.
Sorry for being morbid
but I can't help but think
we are at the mercy of an unknown clock,
constantly on the brink.
Friends and family
have been ripped away from me
and if I had a little more courage,
maybe I'd have a little more peace.
Your ego is your
biggest cockblock
but I'm begging you to
set it aside
just for a moment,
ears wide.
You moved me
when I was unable.
You kissed me
and I found I'm capable.
I will not take it upon myself to get caught in the reeling.
I will not take it upon myself to assume what you're feeling.
I won't hurt you if that's why you're silent.
Stop keeping it in the back of your mind.
Can we find an alignment?
If I die tomorrow
I would never know what you thought of me.
And I find that a great shame to us and to our history.

THE MARCHING BAND

Are we a ticking time bomb?
Sorry I've had a short fuse.
Tears come out of me like waterfalls
and I have no good excuse.
Maybe I'm broken,
but I'll clasp to you closely
no matter how slowly insecurity
creeps in when you hold me.
Give me your kisses and
your chaos and your breath
'cause without your world of color,
my life is dull and bereft.
I want your joy.
I want your shame.
I'll adore your quirks
and I'll honor your pain.
I crave all of you
in the marrow of my splintered bones.
I've waited so long to find you,
resting on your sternum is now home.
I don't wanna fight anymore,
believe the words on this page.
You and I are the greatest story alive,
one I could never dream to erase.
I promise to give you more
and I'll do whatever it takes.
My heart beats like a drum for you,
it will beat till the mallet breaks.
With your dark brown curls
and lavender in your eyes,
I want this music forever.
I don't care if it's a long time.

FLASH FLOOD

I piled it up so high.
I didn't think anything would get through.
What I built was impermeable,
it was strong,
it was permanent,
so I thought.
It all came so suddenly
and the dam I had worked
so hard to construct
broke within a matter of seconds.

I should have known better.
You do that to me you know?
You break everything I build.
You've broken everything I've built.

Engulfed by my
adoration,
fear,
anxiety,
curiosity,
lust,
hope,
paranoia,
emptiness,
ecstasy.

You do that to me you know.
You have a way of
making me feel
everything all at once.

FOR KEVIN

He bought me ice cream.
Lavender honeycomb.
And it was one of the sweetest things
I've ever had the pleasure of tasting.
He opened my car door
and extended his hand
so I wouldn't fall.
He called me beautiful.
He asked to see my play
even though I wouldn't be on stage,
but rather in a booth
making lights shift
and praying the actors didn't screw up.
He took me to the train station,
kissed my cheek goodbye,
"See you in New York!"
he said.

I left
with wet eyes
thinking of the things
my father never did.
Not because he didn't have the chance.
Not because he didn't have the capacity.
Because he didn't want to.
There's a gap in a daughter's mind
when her father abuses and abandons her,
leaving a broken body behind.

As the years go by
the void gets smaller,
yet the strange need to fill it
never escapes.
But in two days together,
your father filled a sliver
of the hollowness I've carried,
and will continue to carry,
my whole life.

A sliver was enough.

JUNE

color me in crimson red
kisses like violin strings on my neck
keep playin' me till I'm out of tune
you're warmer than the hottest day in the month of June
in you go, I giggle not 'cause it's funny
I'm just full of joy, you stick like the sweetest honey
a fever burnin' between my thighs
felt so good, I almost cried
shallow breaths and cotton candy tongues
plunge me into the deep,
no song left unsung

GOODBYE JOHN WAYNE

Goodbye John Wayne.
You've been good to me.
Eleven years I've stayed,
now it's time for me to leave.
Thank you for your love,
thank you for your time.
All the lessons I've learned here
helped me discover what's mine.
I see my apartment complex below
and the local shopping mart.
I see my high school theater
where I made the purest art.
I spot the tennis courts
where I learned how to be a good sport,
where I became a champion, won a medal
and where I also fell short.
I get a glimpse of the Dicken's neighborhood
where I fell off an unhinged inflatable slide,
scraped half my face off on the asphalt,
shocked my skull didn't crack wide.
I grimace at the El Camino cul-de-sac
where someone I loved betrayed me.
But across the street are the fairgrounds,
one of the most beautiful sights I would ever see.
The church down the street is lit up
as the kids tumble on the playground.
That church helped me find my voice,
I fell in love with the sound.
I see the pools of homes
where cast parties and kissing collided.
I replay the funeral of my teacher's lost baby,
forever wishing her grief subsided.
I've become all I am here,
in this little town I've grown.
I'm frightened for what comes next,
you're all I have ever known.

THIS IS NOT A LOVE LETTER.

I know.
It's superfluous and you hate that.
I say it to every human,
child,
friend,
dog,
object,
good idea,
piece of art,
Bon Iver song
and sometimes,
to strangers.
But to you?
No.
Those three words won't suffice.
They won't mean anything.
So here's my attempt
to find something that will.

You're a one hundred piece orchestra
tuning their instruments before a performance
and the thunderous roll of applause
as the curtain falls.
You are the knot in my stomach
when I skip a step on a flight of stairs
and the immediate relief I feel
when I realize I didn't break something.
You are the Nevadan snowcapped mountains
when I visit my family in the winter
and the warmth of hot chocolate
that goes down my throat.
You are the spark of a match
and the fresh smell of charcoal when it's blown out.
You are the wind while my body dances
out of a car's sunroof through the jungles of Hawaii
and the imminent sunburn that follows.
You are the rumble of the plane before it takes off the runway.
You are a suspension pedal on a Steinway playing D major.
You are the comfort of warm laundry.
You are in the glass of every train window I've ever looked through.
You are the ink that flows out of a pen when I sign my name.
You are a ferris wheel stopped at its apex while everything below is in motion.

You are the petals on a rose when they are in full bloom.
You are the petals on a rose when they fall.
There's beauty in the fall.

You should know by now
that I will never say to you
what I say to everyone else.
But I hope that maybe,
just maybe,
I said something better.

Act II

The Reckoning

SURPRISE

Love has arrived at my doorstep.
It has bleach blonde hair now
with darkest brown at the root
and hazel eyes that glisten in the morning and in the dark.
It has gemstones on its hands
and gold in its ears
and a taste of sarcasm on its tongue when it doesn't get its way.

Love has arrived at my doorstep.
It smells of oranges and cedar
and it wears denim tightly around its waist
and it has crass jokes that know no bounds.
It has thin, round glasses
and moles around its mouth
and the most beautiful smile
when it allows itself to show.

Love has arrived at my doorstep.
It clanks its bracelets against my body
with exaggerated gestures
and it speaks clumsy words
and it always tries to do its best.
It never fails to make me laugh
and does so till my ribs ache
and that is worth everything to me
when laughter is what I need the most.

Love has arrived at my doorstep
and it's not what I could have ever imagined it looking like.
It's better.

And now I don't know what to do.

RAINBOW DYNAMITE

You used it
to blast my heart open
until its bits and pieces
were scattered,
splattered,
across my walls,
across the country.

Reds
and blues
and yellows
and greens.
An entire rainbow
burst inside of me.

You ruined my plan
with a plane ticket in your hand
and I thought maybe
this is how it could be.

Reds
and blues
and yellows
and greens.
An entire rainbow burst
inside of me.

HAPPY HALLOWEEN

You hate today.
The guys are buffoons,
the girls show too much
and everybody wants to go home with somebody,
except the people they go home with make them feel
lonelier than when the night began.
I took myself out to a bar.
My hair at my waist,
black tank-top, jeans
and baby blue cowboy boots.
I wore myself for a costume since
the rest of the characters were already taken,
but if you gave me a mirror
I wouldn't recognize who I was.
Mickey Mouse was curbside, smoking a cigarette.
The Pope was puking and
Antony and Cleopatra were having a big fucking fight.
I think they broke up.
The DJ played Red Hot Chili Peppers.
"Step from the road, to the sea to the sky,
and I do believe what we rely on…"

I thought about
not relying on you anymore
so I left the dance floor.
I went down to the basement
to find the bathroom where
a woman was vomiting,
another was kissing her lover
and the last was crying.

I left, went to a bodega off 1st and A
and bought myself a candy bar.
I chewed on it slowly
as I walked back home
to write this poem
for you.

MAROONED

I'm losing my grit,
losing my steam,
as thousands of people
all around me
are moving,
are breathing,
are chasing a dream
while I fantasize about you
and what we could be
and this distraction
has made my body so heavy,
now I'm swallowed up,
a stranger forever lost in your sea.

CLAY PIGEON

Down,
down,
down.
Shredded parts of me
plunge into the ground.

One by one,
bits disregarded,
making this bird
an easy target.

Love is molded by the shape of hands.
I just hope my wings will be able to withstand
being the inevitable victim of sport.

CLEMENTINE

Peeled back,
sweet
juice drips
tenderly
down my chin
and as I wipe my face
and lick my fingers,
I can't stop thinking about you
being inside me.

QUILTING

Inch by inch,
square by square,
trying to stitch my life together,
but you are everywhere.
In my hair,
in my clothes,
can't escape your grasp,
not even in these poems.
Don't know when you became my world,
yet here we are,
but as the days go by
I get more and more far
away from your lips,
away from your hands,
away from your dreams,
away from your plans.
Now I'm holding this
tattered quilt in my arms,
but you're the only one
with the needle and the yarn.

NIAGARA FALLS

The smell of winter pines,
the burning of the snow.
Your hands fold into mine,
don't wanna let go.

Humming sweet melodies,
lingering on the path.
Water flows around us
at an incomprehensible mass.

Adoring all that you are
with Christmas lights around your neck.
Your hazel-eyed winks
leave me an absolute wreck.

With kisses of rainbow light
and mist caressing my face,
one look at you and I've decided
this is my favorite place.

BIRTHDAY CANDLES

Twelve to be exact.
Couldn't fit the thirteenth,
even though you turned twenty-four.
I couldn't mess up your perfect name in icing.
So I hope the twelve were enough.
I hope the burn was enough because
when you hit the seventeenth buzzer,
I seared my thumb with my lighter
and luckily I couldn't feel a thing.
I was two glasses of gin in.
I couldn't comprehend that you were here at my door
and you were about to blow out your birthday candles
when you kissed me on the mouth
and we both forgot about the cake.
The burning in my bed
was more important.

HERSHEY

Snow falling from the sky,
your warm hands on my thighs,
sighs in our mouths,
in our eyes
and you're tired from your flight
'cause this feels so right
as Manhattan morning light
holds our bodies together,
yours and mine,
kisses stain like red wine
(let's never scrub them out)
let's keep walking this line
because your mouth tastes better
than this Hershey bar I bite
as I hold you while you sleep
and nothing between us feels far
anymore.

BULLETPROOF VEST

You sport it like a tattoo.
The material's never thin.
Nothing will scrape, let alone unearth
that metallic muscle under your skin.
You've been hurt before.
Too afraid to let me in.
Lack of vulnerability
is the competition you strive to win.
This is a familiar dance,
back and forth I spin.
Your heart is so hard
while mine tries to grin.
Now here I am, raw,
open and warm from within
but how can I stay when
what's strapped to your chest
won't let us begin.

LINENS

I messed up the sheets
on my side of the
mattress,
again.

They keep riding up
no matter how
hard I try to keep
them down.

The weight of my body
isn't enough, so I will continue to
shove them down aggressively
with my hands.

But don't be angry about the sheets.

For the more we make love,
the more unkempt the bed.

GROCERY BAG

I'm strapped over her shoulder
and I'm pressing everything I am into her.
Two gallons of milk,
a gallon of water,
a carton of orange juice,
a bag of clementines,
four apples,
spinach,
eggs,
carrots,
hummus,
ketchup,
a loaf of bread,
peanut butter,
a jar of jam
and a bouquet of her favorite flowers — peonies.
Her drive is quite commendable,
but she's an idiot.
She thinks that as a "real" New Yorker,
she can pile all of her grocery items
into me
and only me?
Just a blue, ninety-nine cent IKEA bag
she brought from California
because of my dependable sturdiness?
I relent.
This woman thinks that her limbs
won't give out going up these four flights.
Two trips are not for the weak honey.
In fact, they're essential to avoid bruised shoulder blades.
She took thirty minutes just to get inside.
She has done this same routine
about eleven or twelve times
and I am pretty worn out,
but she's the most tenacious woman I've ever met.

Until everything collapses
out from under her
as she pants up the final flight.
The stairs drip in condiments as she stands in her loneliness.

Finally,
we're both

completely and utterly
broken.

TIDAL WAVES

This undertow is a familiar place
and I'm tired of
salt on my tongue,
empty lungs
and your overwhelmed face.
Can you glide on
the tidal waves that crash
on your chest
because what I have for you is relentless,
unabashed
and inevitably
I'll always come back.
Each break is
more intense than the last
but the release is too beautiful,
so I hold steadfast.

GALA APPLE

Go get high with that girl you just met
'cause smoking pot takes precedence over consoling your pet.
Your best friend's here crying on the line
and with my shaking hands, somehow yours are the ones tied.
Lost my spine
trying to make you mine.
You're a paradox with no heart,
just a body that walks,
that wanders
through life without concern
if others talk
about how you break
and continue to break them.
I understand I'll never be yours,
though I wanted you all mine,
so I ate the apple you left me behind.
Needed that final taste
of the parts that I gave
but when I bit into the red,
I realized it was all a waste.

FOR ME

Make no mistake,
none of this is for you.
Yes you helped me get here
and for that I'm eternally grateful,
but this is what I needed to do
to help me heal.
It was all for me.
In return,
maybe you'll heal too.

That's the beautiful thing about poetry.
Everybody assumes it's about them.
And because of that
it's for everyone.

(MI.) TO NEW YORK CITY 2

Put your sword down.
The battle is over.
You can rest now.
Your enemy has fled
the territory.
My white flag
is waving high
across the country.

How I wish you could see me.
How I wish you would forgive me.

WHEN I SAW YOU AT MY SILL

Three years ago,
on a warm October night
my ankle was wrapped tight
in bandages
from falling down a flight
in my home.
Broken bone
and all alone,
I almost reached for my phone,
then I saw you.
I reached for my crutches instead,
not because my ankle needed support
but because my heart cascaded in a way
never before.
It hit the floor
when you knocked on my door
and it was then
I was sure,
that in this cataclysm
I loved you more
than anyone
I have ever loved
before.

THE WOOLGATHERER

It's the middle of January.
The snow is falling hard.
It runs into the window against my back,
accompanied by the bass of the party next door
and I think of where we were
last January
when you joined acting class again
and I couldn't look at you
without wanting to cry.
You remember?
Caressing my warm hands,
formulating Mastrosimone's poetry
as you poured it into my being?
You held my shaking body against the makeshift door frame
and my objective was to leave you,
but I ended up letting you stay.
And it was real.
Then the applause came
and the wooden floor caught my gaze
and my tears because
I was loving you on display
and you were
just acting.
Now my knees are curled up to my chest
on my twin size bed
and the snowflakes are crashing against the glass
and I'm crashing into the relentless reminders
that I left California.
I left summer skies.
I left your cotton candy mouth
and I wonder if it's best for me
to let go.

GRACE IS A VIOLENT PROCESS

Do you hate that I went after what I wanted?
Do you hate that it happened to be you
and that everything around you started to crumble
when I started to shake you?
I was there
picking at your rubble
just trying to touch something
you've touched.
I was praying you wouldn't detest me
for groveling.
I couldn't help wanting you
and I bulldozed anyone in my way.
How I wish
I could have been more patient
and more kind
and more selfless
but I wasn't.
You brought out
a darkness in me
because I was so broken.
You had to fucking squint
to see the crack where
the light came in.

But I promise
it was worth it.
I'm worth it.
And the next time
I want to cause an earthquake,
I promise there'll be no casualties.

NECTAR

We're at your aunt's house
and I'm sitting on the couch
with sunburnt shoulders, sipping green tea
while Tim fingers the tune of Blackbird on
his guitar. I hear the birds singing along
from the patio while you're playing the piano poorly.
The entire scene makes me smile.

Sarah just graduated with her Master's
and is tipsy off a strong Bloody Mary
that tasted like ketchup, so I stole sips of your mimosa
and left my red lips all over your glass.
I wasn't sorry about it.

We played games on the grass in the backyard
and I got a little too competitive and
accidentally hit your aunt in the ankles.
Thankfully she forgave me. I know this because
she still let me partake in her perfectly crumbled baked brie.

As I take all of this goodness in,
I find myself wanting this life
with you and them and my ballooned heart
is ready to burst.
This sweetness is all-consuming.
I'm afraid that if I get too hasty,
it'll sting like this red all over me.

NEW YEAR'S EVE

You're on your plane
and I'm on the JFK air train
and I've missed my stop.
I go around once more
and I don't mind because
I have nowhere to go
and being on this train is the closest
I'll be to you
for quite
some time.
I stopped looking for my exit long ago.
Look at that.
I think I see you taking off.

An hour goes by
and I decide it's time
to go home.
I hop from air train to subway
all alone.
I put in my headphones
to drown out the lovers
I see getting ready to celebrate tonight.
Glittered eyes and sequined dresses,
red lipstick smeared on cheeks,
longing to be under a disco ball,
confetti over you and me.
The clock would strike twelve
and you'd put your mouth on mine
and we wouldn't have to feel like
we ran out of time.

But my phone dies
and the music stops.
I'm exiting the subway and
down 9th I walk.
I pass the bodega on my corner,
grab a gallon of milk
(peanut butter M&M's too).
It's your favorite beverage
and though I stopped drinking dairy years ago,
tonight I celebrate you.

THOUGHTS FROM UNDER THE BROOKLYN BRIDGE

It started with a kiss
on a coffee table.
Though it was only acting,
something remained stable.
Had no clue how to deal,
how to fight,
how to show,
we entered through the mouth of summer
and into the bosom of autumn we go.

Time went on.
You met others,
while I was still around
clutching to your covers.
Writhing in pain
needing something to throw,
we entered through the mouth of summer
and into the bosom of autumn we go.

I saw you grappling with being alone.
You caught me red-handed wanting to make you moan.
You were my prey
and I attacked real low,
we entered through the mouth of summer
and into the bosom of autumn we go.

Thrilled I was selfish
and drank you down like wine.
I knew I'd miss you too much,
but I pretended I was fine.
Years went by,
my heart black as a crow,
we entered through the mouth of summer
and into the bosom of autumn we go.

Now I'm far away
and needing your heat.
The warmth of June
is now November's cold on my feet.
Hoping you won't find another
above or below,
we entered through the mouth of summer
and into the bosom of autumn we go.

Let's just grow
and go away together.
You taste of brown sugar,
please stay forever.
Let's say the things
we've always wanted to know.
We entered through the mouth of summer
and into the bosom of autumn,

we go.

LAUNDRY DAY

You just had to
spray your cologne
all over my clothes
in my suitcase
before I left California,
so I would know
that you're with me
even when you're not.

I'm not so sure
I want to be reminded of that anymore.
I've gotta stop writing for you
and go get my quarters.
Sometimes the machines get full
and I can't risk that.

Not this time.

SOUNDBOARD FOR SORROW

Listen,
listen,
listen.
It's what I do best.
I'm always there for you to get something
off your chest.
What about me, huh?
When is it my turn?
I'm just another cross to bear.
Another bridge to burn.
I wonder if I make you happy
deep within your bones
or if you only desire me
to feel less alone.
Most people confuse love for fear.
They might be the same.
Both can make you crazy,
both can make you ashamed.
But I will not be
your soundboard for sorrow.
My heart isn't something you can just borrow.
You know I'll always come around,
like water to a mill.
I feel for you deeply.
Always have,
always will.

03.13.20

I'll never forget how it felt
when the wheels of the plane
scraped against the tarmac.
With a smile from ear to ear,
I raced through the airport
knowing that just around the corner,
there you'd be
greeting me,
fresh from the city.
Little did I know
I'd catapult into your arms
and you'd never let go.

HOMETOWN

Splitting a chicken sandwich and fries
in a booth at 3:42 am
with us and our waiters in masks
while triple digit heat
waits patiently for us outside,
wasn't exactly how I pictured our first morning
in my hometown together.
I would have shown you
the Grand Canyon
and there would have been a picnic waiting for us
at the top with chocolate-covered strawberries
and a valley of vastness below.
I would have shown you the
greatest water parks
and you would have helped me apply
twenty layers of sunblock as the concrete
burnt the bottoms of our feet.
I would have brought you to my favorite
childhood diner and we would have eaten
my favorite breakfast sausage patties
and drank virgin Shirley Temples
and I'd make a poor attempt to
tie a knot in the cherry stem.
We would have driven by the neighborhood
where I was raised and
where I was bruised from an early age
from racing downhill on my
electric scooter
and from other injuries
I cannot tell you yet.
You would have seen the house
that is no longer mine
but has built me into the woman I am
and it would have been so
strange to see it for the first time
in over ten years.
But I would have wanted to.
I like sharing my life with you,
even the ugliest parts.
I would have taken you to airplane park
and we would watch the planes fly
over our heads as we lie on our backs on the grass
and I would have cried because the last time I did that I was eight

and I was with a stranger called my father.
I would have shown you the
amber sunsets in
the city of Summerlin.
There's nothing more gorgeous
than a desert sunset.

On our way home
after our twenty-four hour trip to Nevada,
we caught the last bit of light.
As the baby blue turned to violet
and the violet turned to navy blue,
I couldn't help myself.
I only stared at you.

Act III

The Salvaging

PROLOGUE

I see palm trees out of the small window
I've cracked to release steam
from this shower I'm taking to rinse you
out of my hair and off my body
into the drain and as the drain
starts to clog I'm reminded
how I was beginning the fulfilling
of a life I always wanted
but then the grocery stores
were bombarded by greed
and all of the beautiful marquees
went dark and my heart followed.
Then the hospitals started to overflow
and makeshift morgues were only a block away
and everything began to fill up
and continues to fill with bodies
and bodies
and bodies
and I continued to fill with fear,
so I fled,
only to stand
in different empty aisles
on a different coast
and now the drain is backed up
because I'm ankle-deep
in my own failures
but I look at the trees
and I slowly start to breathe
and I see how they sway under the Los Angeles sun
and I'm reminded that this pandemic will pass,
this water will drain
and that home is no longer a place outside,
but rather within me.

THE PRECIPICE OF OURSELVES

This is where we find out exactly who we are as people
and I can't tell if that's more heartening or harrowing.
We'll either hit jagged boulders on the way down and crack into oblivion
or we'll land and find ourselves among a field of flowers.

MOLDY BREAD

It's funny how we suddenly find use for things
when they're threatened to be taken away from us.
It was expired past two years.
It was frozen.
It was taking up valuable space where
a tub of my favorite ice cream could be stored instead.

So, yes.
It was I
who threw away the bread.
And of course,
I knew you would find it
in the garbage.
And of course,
you dug it out
and said you wanted to keep it.
You're not one to squander food.
I've known this as long as I've known you.

I should have known better.
Old, moldy and frozen Dave's bread.
"I'll eat it!" you said.
"I won't let it go to waste!" you said.
I think I need to see you clearer.
Instead of focusing on how
you don't let go of things,
maybe I should start focusing
on how tightly you hold onto them.

URINARY TRACT INFECTIONS

Can't have sex again —
fuck a UTI.
I hate crying my eyes out
in the middle of the night.
You're off in dreamland
and I'm curled up on the couch
holding my knees to my chest
like a baby kangaroo in its mother's pouch.
Can't afford this pain anymore,
but one-seventy-five is worth your touch.
Raged I don't have health insurance,
out-of-pocket antibiotics are really testing my luck.
Could have kidney failure
or my sugar addiction got out of hand.
I wanna go back to a simpler time
like a small child playing in the sand.
But here I am unemployed 'cause
real life socked me in the face.
I feel like a failure, a dumbass
a complete waste of space,
all while I'm pissing orange
and having to be sexually cautious
and I'm losing a full night's sleep
'cause my pills make me nauseous.
But at the end of the day
I'm still here with you,
taking me to pharmacies all over town
and holding me till I get through.

THIS WINDOW IS NOT MINE

It's gloomy.
I wish I could see the city skyline
but the Empire State is furthest from my mind.
Instead, these blinds are dusty and the glass is smudged and the
splintered palm trees look like hangnails and I want
to bite them off and spit them out.
I see the off-white and pistachio accented apartments across the way.
Letters "A" and "B" on the front doors.
The neighbor's barbecue is closed.
The pile of mail outside remains untouched.
Usually the children play on the tiny patch of grass out front.
Today isn't one of those days.

I'M THE KNIGHT IN SHINING ARMOR

White cloth
drapes from my ceiling
and surrounds my bed frame.
It makes me feel like a princess
and it protects me from bugs
so they don't fly into my mouth
or up my nose
while I dream
of being another
nine-year-old girl
in a different room.
I dream about everything
because it's going to be better
than what's inevitably about to come.
I stare at the pink detailing
on my bedroom walls,
waiting.

It's early and
he is very angry.
He's spitting
at me to clean my
already spotless room.
I cry.
He swears.
I shouldn't have known what fuck meant.
Even then.

I still think of that morning
and I am forced to remind myself
to be gentle
with my heart and know
that I was just a child,
locked away
in her princess tower
thinking that the man
raging inside
would be her savior.

I am allowed to feel like a princess.
But I don't need a prince to save me when
I've saved myself
many times over.

DEAD POETS ARE ROLLING IN THEIR GRAVES

Dead poets are rolling in their graves.
Whitman, Baldwin, Dickinson, Bukowski (a piece of shit, but a poet nonetheless).
I'm sure they're reeling at todays Instagram girls
taking photographs of their half-naked bodies,
accompanied with advertisements and hashtags
who get to travel across the country with their
perfumes, workout clothes and dietary supplements.
Italy, Paris, Barcelona, Santorini,
where they have the luxury to be paid
to write regurgitated sentences,
into regurgitated paragraphs,
into regurgitated books of poetry
that look like they say so much,
when they don't say anything.
Can we call a white screen
with four mere lines of text
(and maybe a doodle of a flower)
a poem at all?
Who gets to decide?
Who is in charge of all this?
I want to speak with them.
Everything today is about
things, things, things.
Sponsorships for caffeinated beverages or golden rings.
Hemingway said, "Writing is easy. All you do is sit at a typewriter and bleed."
But I guarantee he did not mean this.
Are you bleeding yet?
Are you bleeding yet?
Show me the blood under your nails and in your teeth.
What the fuck is a poem anyway.
My whole life is an unfinished poem,
so please don't listen to me.
I have no authority.
What I do know is that
I will never be a social media poet.
I will never write for the delusional masses.
I have too much empathy to write like the rest of them.
But the grand irony is
I am a girl,
I am a poet
and this poem
is on Instagram.

FLASHING VENICE BOULEVARD

I've always had a funny relationship
with my tits.
They grew early
and on Sundays
the school teachers
secluded me to scorn
my immodesty
and forced me to change into
another baggy t-shirt,
another baggy t-shirt,
another baggy t-shirt,
no matter the fabric,
no matter the color,
no matter the cut,
the flat girl
to my right
was never taken away.
She was never taken out
of Sunday school
in the same exact top
and it was in the same exact moment
when I knew the
shirt wasn't the problem.
The shirt was never the problem.

These thoughts race through my brain
as I flash the entirety of Venice Boulevard
in all of my glory.
I wish those bastards in their
polo ties
and three-piece suits
could see me now,
see how I turned out
to be everything
they hate.

Free.

THE COLOR OF APRIL

Everything was dark blue.
The water, the moon,
me and you.
Never felt sand like ice in the night,
sneaking around like little kids
following the tide.

Everything was dark blue.
The water, the moon,
me and you.
You were oh so cold
and we perched upon the tower.
Yet I've never felt warmer
and more seen at this hour.

Everything was dark blue.
The water, the moon,
me and you.
But people are dying
and I'm trying to find my home.
So much is in my body,
anxiety of the world fills my bones.

Everything was dark blue.
The water, the moon,
me and you.
My eyes look at the sea,
the pier glistens back at me
but your eyes are far brighter,
one look and I'm lucky to breathe.

Everything was dark blue.
The water, the moon,
me and you.
Engulfed in all your beauty,
even in Earth's plight,
has once again confirmed
all that we are is right.

TO THE WOMEN I'VE HURT

I wonder why I rarely leave,
but somehow I am always left.
It's the constant battle of finding myself perfect,
yet an undeniable, selfish fuckup.
I try to love my friends more than I love myself
and in that process I end up loving nothing
as well as I'm capable of.
I'm sorry that when I was cut in half
I felt the need to make halves out of you as well.
I wish I could have had a spine thick enough
so I wouldn't have needed to rely on yours.
I thought that
approval was water
and I was just an empty pot
and my leaves wouldn't spring from the soil
unless somebody else told them to.
I don't know why it took me
this long to grow old and grow up.
I don't know why it took me
this long to look inside myself
only to realize that I hurt you
because I was hurting.

MARCO POLO

"Marco!" I yelled, eyes closed in a deep pool.
"Polo!" the boy replied back, as we began our duel.

"Marco!" I exclaimed, my eleven-year-old body flailing about.
"Polo!" the boy giggled back, no part of him filled with doubt.

"Marco!" I screeched, my legs giving out from the tide.
"Polo!" the boy jeered back, his arms stretched wide.

"Marco!" I cried, as his quick fingers undid my top.
"Polo!" the boy cackled back, he would not stop.

"Mar—co — " hyperventilating, chest bare like he planned.
"Polo!" the boy snickered back leaving the pool, my armor in hand.

"Marco…" I choked on chlorine, unable to use my arms.
"Polo," the boy smiled back, mimicking my harm.

I barely uttered the word, exhausted from this children's game.
The boy glanced back, achieving euphoria from my cold, naked shame.

RATTLESNAKES

No.
Don't do it.
Just hold it all in
until you feel like
throwing up
because it's the higher road,
the kinder path.
It's expected of you
to just stick it
and shove it
until it dies
inside of you,
but that peril
has irreparable
consequences too.
A close friend told me
that you teach people
the way to treat you,
so what happens
when people decide
I've become dirt
and they give themselves
the freedom to take their boots
and grind their grimy heels
into my face?
How
am I the one
constantly expected to
be graceful?
No.
You do not get to use me
to make yourself feel better.
There are some things
I will not tolerate.
Kindness grows deep within me,
that I know.
But I'm allowed to be angry.
I'm allowed to let it show.
And guess what?
I love it.
Rattlesnakes are graceful too.
Step on me again.
I dare you.

TERMS AND CONDITIONS A.

When I was eleven I watched porn for the first time.
I consulted Google.
"Two girls kissing."
It was sublime
and I didn't know why.
I liked boys.
I definitely liked boys
but maybe it's because
that's what I was taught,
but as I grew
I knew
I didn't want to see any boy
underneath his clothes.
It felt different with girls.
It felt safer,
their tender bodies and hearts
alike.
Men are shown violence from
an early age and I feared
it would be brought upon me
and it was.
It always was.
So who was I supposed to turn to
to be held,
to be safe,
to be loved.
I couldn't say the word.
So how could I feel the feeling?
Stuck within the confines
of taking the bread and water,
of being submerged into the sacred bathtub,
of seeing Jesus's hands bleed on the cross,
all for me.
For this fucking sinner.
The last thing I wanted was
an eternity in hell.
So, the women I've never touched,
never kissed,
never held —
those desires still live in me.
Those unlived dreams still lie in me.
I was blinded back then.
Now I'm old enough to see.

MALIBU FIRESIDE

I remember looking at him
on the dance floor with her
and sobbing into your arms
about it for the next three hours.

We left the party and
sat by the fire alone,
wrapped up in a blanket
and it felt like home
'cause you're the truest friend
I've ever known.

We looked at the constellations
and I saw them in your cheeks,
smiling back as you wiped my tears
from that teenage dream-boy who broke me.

Did you know your brown eyes
could make anyone fall into them
like a pool of chocolate?
So of course I'd never want to leave
such a forgiving sweetness.

The fire begins to crackle,
not the one in front of us, but the one inside.
I thought about kissing you woman,
on that warm Malibu night.

LIGHT

It's not just through the blinds,
it's not only from the sun.
It's found in kind hearts,
it's found when it's begun.
It makes the world not so heavy,
it's seen in children's eyes.
It cuts through all the meaningless,
it cuts through all the lies.
It's the laughter of my mother,
it's the first sound she ever heard.
It encompasses all I try to be,
it was my very first word.

FOR JASON

There are many things I want for you
more than I want for myself.
How I wish you could read this poem.
How I wish I could help.
I want to know your mind
and your favorite places to go.
I want us to sit on an airplane
and look at the clouds below.
I want to share a home-cooked meal
from a recipe you made on your own.
I want to see a life you've built,
I want you to have a home.
I want to see you get married
and hold your lover's hand
while I sit weeping in the pews
or sing jubilantly with the band.
I want to tell you my deepest fears
and in return you'd do the same,
then we'd hug ever so closely
and bond through shared pain.
I know you're more than your autism.
I love you as any sister would
and while my wants are boundless,
I wouldn't change you if I could.

I WANT TO SHAVE MY HEAD

I want to shave my head
and not give a damn about it.
I want to walk down the street with bare skin
and not think if people can see the acne scars on my chin.
I want to slick my hair back with pomade
and wear dresses and tuxedos
but not have either of them come with assumptions
pertaining to who I may or may not love.
I want to smile when I think of those who
hurt me.
I want to wish them peace.
I want to get fucked whenever I want and not
worry about getting another UTI.
I want to not care about the girls on the playground
who called me fat in the fifth grade.
I want to pierce my ears three times on each side and
get drawings upon drawings along both of my arms.
I want a perfect, unmarked body because
that's what I was told would get me into heaven.
I want to ride a bicycle and not have flashbacks
of the time I crashed into a pole and bled all over the sidewalk.
I want to not care about the man who molested me.
I want to own my failures and my fuckups
and my successes and my glory.
I want to be an irreplaceable human being.
I want to be a damn good writer.
But most of all,
I want to make you feel something.

NO EXPECTATIONS FOR THE BROKEN

How could I have expected you to see me
when you were blinded by your own ignorance.
Why did I think you could hold me close
when you weren't comfortable holding
your own two hands.
You're on me like a bandage.
The wound is deep that misses you.
I remember the way you laughed
and the brilliance of your acting.
I thought to myself,
"She has the world at her fingertips."
I will never know why you left me
with no answer.
But I know one day you'll have your stage
and your name up in lights.
I'll be looking up at your marquee,
even if you do not remember me.

How could I have expected you to care for me
when you were taught that the most important person is you.
Why did I think you would care if I cried
when you mistake tears for frailty and vulnerability for shame.
I still remember that day you left for San Diego
full of rage and an internal mess.
You said terrible things
but I helped you and brought
your suitcase down anyway.
That's how I was raised.
I thought to myself,
"She's in pain so it's okay
if she's the battering ram
because I'm tough enough.
I won't splinter away."
I will never know why you were so unkind to me.
But I know one day you'll make something of yourself
and realize that you don't have to make people feel small
to be grand.

How could I have expected you to hear me
when you were drowning in your own thoughts.
Why did I think you would show up for me
when you weren't able to give yourself the gift of you.
I still hold you tightly in my chest.

I remember that cold day in the museum
when we were walking separately,
marveling at the gorgeous work in front of our eyes.
I thought to myself,
"One day, you could have your own Whitney."
I will never know why I was unable to help you.
I know one day you'll have your gallery.
I hope you'll cut that ribbon
and get everything you deserve and more,
even if I'm not witnessing your greatness like we had planned.

How could I have expected you to speak to me
when you were afraid of your own voice.
Why did I think you could communicate
when you were told from an early age
that you were always wrong.
It's been two years.
I'm still here.
I remember the day your mother
slammed the door in my face
and I begged her to give you
the flowers I bought
as an apology,
even though I didn't know what I was sorry for.
But I know one day you'll find your voice
and tell your mother how you feel
and when that day comes,
I hope it's the best day of your life.
I want that for you.
I really do.

FORREST GUMP

"Please don't grope me in my sleep."
I told him a thousand times over.
(Yes, he was my lover, my first —
don't worry.)
But many others
weren't.
(That, my lover did not know.)
Some would slide
their slimy hands
into places they did not belong
and I cried because I
never understood why
they thought my body belonged to them.
It must have been my favorite pair of pink shorts.
I wore those too much.

At seventeen,
I woke one morning
to a friend's

.

.

.

to a friend's
hand in my
underwear
after falling asleep on the couch
after a late night
viewing of Forrest Gump.
I screamed in horror
to demand what was wrong with him
but no words came out,
just hollow sounds
as he withdrew his hand out of my baby blue ice cream cone undies.
"Sorry, it's just my biological instincts."

.

.

.

My brain scratched like a broken record and I was too paralyzed
to replay it.
Did he just say that?
He couldn't have.
My naiveté had ran my body into the ground like a construction drill.
It was too late to have

wished I had worn a helmet.
But nobody could have protected
this Mormon raised and milky-skinned teenager
from the monsters called men who are not taught consent.

He asked to drive me home
and I reluctantly agreed since I didn't want
a river to flow from my eyes
for all the world to see
for a forty-five minute stroll.

I wanted to crash the car
with every passing traffic light.
But I didn't.
I wanted to go back months later to that shitty cul-de-sac
and tell his little brother why I didn't visit anymore,
then proceed to key the Mercedes he did not earn.
But I didn't.
I wanted to gauge out his amber eyes and shove them into his
mother's skull so she could see firsthand, the man he turned out to be.
I wanted to tell my mother why my cheeks were red and puffy like a cherub angel
and explain why I slept until seven in the evening that day.
But I didn't.

I should have.

I should have told my lover
this is why
I didn't own a pair of shorts, even though we live in Southern California.
I should have told my lover
this is why
I sometimes flinched at his touch and said it was too much.
I should have told my lover
that I was sorry I couldn't explain.
I should have told my lover
this is why I fucking
hate Forrest Gump.

TERMS AND CONDITIONS B. — DRIPPING IN ICE, VISIONS OF GOLD AND COMMITTING TO THINGS YOU NEVER KNEW

It all started with an oath.
caressed in my hands
and heavy on my shoulders.
at this tender age,
I could barely keep
my Tamagotchi alive
so how could I expect
my little self to keep a
lifetime of promises
to the Almighty one
and his only begotten Son.
my hands weren't big enough
to carry this weight
but into the water I went anyways
because that's what you were
supposed to do.
obey at all costs.
not getting ex-communicated on
my eight-year-old watch.
I walked
step by step,
clutching the golden rail
of the baptismal font.
my pure white jumpsuit stuck
to my body like a leech as
I moved like molasses and I thought
this is what suffocating feels like.
I am David.
this water is Goliath.
submerged into the ice I went.
I felt the bubbles
from my exhale surround me
and I wished that
I never had to resurface,
for I had just achieved perfection.
I'm spotless.
that's me now.
it was all downhill from here.
I should have held my breath
longer.
I didn't know
I was holding myself to

never having coffee,
never laughing jubilantly while taking a hit,
never having a talisman permanently pressed into my skin,
never making love outside of wedlock,
never making love to a woman, even inside wedlock
(also off the table)
never fucking swearing,
never even entertaining the idea that I didn't want children,
never having a life outside of the box I was shoved into
at an age where it was impossible
to comprehend what it all
meant.
I now know that this was the perfect age.
my limbs weren't fully grown.
I couldn't pry myself out.
vindictive.
the very thing my religion claimed
not to be.
this list, only a sliver
of the commitments
my blooming
mind,
body,
and soul
was making.
and to who?
to God?
to my family?
to myself?
this did not feel
like it was meant for me.
it felt like it was for an idea,
an entity,
or for profit,
or for greed.
all things
I had no interest in.
have no interest in.
I am David.
I now see the real beast.
Goliath has money and flashes corporate teeth.

I think I'm an atheist now.
I sometimes dream about my baptism
and wonder if my life would be simpler
if I hadn't left The Church.

I laugh at my stupid question because
the obvious answer is yes.
who doesn't love a plan.
who doesn't love the idea of being reborn again
or having your own planet
or knowing you'll be reunited with your family
once your body's expired,
retired from our gorgeous mother Earth.
it makes complete sense.
and for those who need that sort of comfort,
that's alright.
we just have different definitions
of comfort.
I'm grateful for those
promises I made at the age of eight.
but I'm even more grateful
I chose not to keep them.

A BAD CASE OF TRICHOTILLOMANIA

I have ripped out my eyelashes
for as long as I can remember.
I would yank out anywhere from
ten to twenty lashes on each eye
on any given day.
It became my source of comfort.
My little secret.
I started to tear
at the front of my scalp until
I would bleed and shortly after that,
I was bald at the
crown of my head.
It felt so good,
no matter how ugly
it looked.

I didn't realize until I was much older
that I only ripped things out from the root
because I was scared
of growing.

TRUCK STOP

I saw a flipped over semi on my way to Georgia
and I wondered if it was you.
I thought about it the entire drive
and if it was you,
I don't think you made it out alive.
I remember you showing me
the interior of your new home,
birthed from a costly divorce.
I was only nine
and I couldn't help but cry
even though you're the one who put
yourself there.
You're the only one to blame
for things never being the same.
I love the world.
I hate being a traveler
because I always think of you on the open road.
So I go for the supercut
of me falling in the pool at two-years-old.
You jumped in with all of your clothes on for me
and I, of course, thought it meant you loved me
but you were only pretending to be the hero
when I was the most wide-eyed and incapable.
Suddenly your cape didn't work.
I outgrew being younger,
you started to show your true colors,
started slipping, spending nights with lovers
that were not my flesh and blood of a perfect mother.
I slept on deflated air mattresses of
the Valium induced mistresses I had mistaken
for your friends,
but I was a child
and I went along
even when something felt wrong —

and then it happened to me.

Green pastures pass me by,
you're yanking out my baby teeth,
pliers in my mouth, screaming open wide.
I hated you inside,
when you went inside
and took away everything

and made me remember to
shut the fuck up and hide.
There was a long time
I wanted to die.
My mother couldn't know.
She wouldn't survive.

And that was the first and only time
I ever underestimated her.

Light slices through the maple trees,
I see you staring back at me.
You're in my vessel
and I want you gone.
I clasp my fists
and force myself to remember
you don't exist
like a mastodon,
but I knew this all along.
I know that I am strong
and I always have and always will belong
to me.

THE PUREST FORM OF DOMINANCE

Like a newborn baby,
you have no defenses.
Here you are and you must
yield to whatever comes your way.
Unable to articulate,
you are helpless
and any response you can think of
will die before it escapes
your pearly white picket fence.
I own you on this page
and from here on out,
you are no more.

YOU ARE NOT THE WORST THING THAT'S EVER HAPPENED TO YOU

The line between having nothing
and everything at the same time
is a line I walk often
and I walk it fine.

How do I take my pain
and put it away in the dark?
So I don't have to face it,
so I won't see the mark.

My body has been fractured
but I'm finally starting to heal.
I was tired of being part of their plan.
Tired of letting them steal.

So I made a plan of my own.
To never allow someone who hurt me,
to never allow someone who claimed me,
define me.

I claim myself.
I love myself too.
I am not the worst thing that's ever happened to me.
Neither are you.

BLOW ME

I've always led with
my hips when I walked.
I enter a room
and I own my ideas and thoughts.
I spread my legs wide
on the subway for comfort.
But I am not a man.

I scarf down a burger and fries
and burp unapologetically afterwards.
I cut off all my hair
because everyone
told me not to.
I slither like a snake
and strike quickly when I want a lover.
But I am not a man.

I am loud and often told to
shut up
but I don't listen.
I laugh like I tell the funniest jokes
and everyone else should be taking notes.
I may not drive a fancy car
but I bet I could make your woman
ride me.
But I am not a man.

I have a hunger for power,
a resilience to pain.
Nothing to lose,
everything to gain.
When I get on my knees
you'll never be the same.
I want you to blow me.
I'm like you, I've got no shame.

I learned to speak with reckless abandon.
That gift, you inherited.
It took me years to practice this craft.
Everything I have, I damn well merited.

FAKE NEWS

god is fake news,
heaven is fake news,
neither is real,
no such thing as payin' dues

the bible is fake news,
congregations are fake news,
jesus isn't real,
he didn't come to save you

baptisms are fake news,
repentance is fake news,
wish I had known this sooner,
woulda saved time cryin' the blues

bishops, popes and priests are fake news,
prophets, seers and revelators are fake news,
because when I was an innocent child
a man endowed by god showed me his real views

all lives matter is fake news,
anti-abortionists and homophobes are fake news,
religious people claim to love all
but we know they pick and choose

so don't come to me
using your king as an excuse,
preaching in the name of your god
is the epitome of fake news.

YOU WERE PUT ON EARTH TO MAKE

I'm enamored with the theater
for reasons held since I was young.
I relish in how plays make me feel.
I fall in love, weep and come undone.

So I chose to learn the craft
from a very early age.
I've spent my entire life
being up high on a stage.

Seventeen shows done in high school,
I was ready to take on the world.
So college here I come,
I'm no longer a little girl.

Now I'm a freshman admit
starting all anew.
This time feels different,
a little fish in a big pool.

But I know I've got grit
and can claw my way above,
so audition after audition
I flew like a dove.

Got a few shows now
under my collegiate belt.
Here comes my fourth,
it's the most nervous I've ever felt.

This play had no structure.
This play had no plan.
It was called "devising"
but I was ready to take a stand.

Day one: we form a circle,
the director states her name.
Says she will be creating the world.
We are just part of her game.

My stomach caved in.
Something wasn't right.
She had a villainous look

between her cobalt eyes.

But who was I to speak?
A newly freshman bee.
This play was for a letter grade,
"Don't rock the boat. Stay unseen."

Day two: we start to work.
Tedious, brutal movements
caused me to sweat through my t-shirt
but it's okay. I know what it's worth.
This is the theater. It's what I deserve.

But improv turned to madness
in the matter of a week.
A girl in my cast chose to hunt me,
for I was much too meek.

She had flaming red hair
and smoked a pack a day.
She was a mother of a young girl
who I felt bad for each passing day.

Then it became my turn
during an improv game one day.
In this game she was the leader
and I had to do whatever she'd say.

I entered the space frightened.
She feasted her blackened eyes.
"Get on all fours, you're my chair now."
My body froze at her reply.

Feeling like an animal
I wanted to cower and go,
wishing for my cast or the crew or the director
to intervene and say no.

They all met me with blank stares
while this leader is ready to lurk.
I pleaded one last time to the director.
"Just do it. It's part of the work."

So on all fours I went,
sucking up salted tears.
She pressed all her weight into my spine

and told everyone to laugh and jeer.

This is an actress
who used me to build her throne,
using theatre as a scapegoat
to make her prey her own.

I'm disgusted by artists
who enact power-hungry fantasies,
using improv as a disguise
for their unique method of brutality.

But she was not an artist
and she will never be.
She's forever stuck in an abyss,
a prisoner to her unkind sea.

I may not be perfect.
I may not have it all right.
But one thing I've got going
is humility and emotional foresight.

I've gone on to be a director now.
I've sold out all my shows.
Turns out fostering a kind environment
only fuels artistic growth.

So never let anybody
bend you until you break.
Cling tightly to those dreams my dear,
you were put on earth to make.

WHERE ARE THE RAZOR BUMPS?

Where are the razor bumps
along the inner thighs of women
in the magazines?
Why are they deemed worthy,
smooth-skinned and flawless
beauty queens?

I know they are not exempt
from this pain that I endure,
because they grow hair down there too
but have the privilege of being demure.

I saw a girl being shamed at the pool one day.
How I wish I had grown a spine.
Everyone mocked her growing garden
until her cheeks flushed and she started crying.

Though we were only thirteen,
I still knew it was wrong
but I was embarrassed of my growing body,
so I just played along.

I wonder where that girl is now.
Wish I could apologize.
Wish I could say, "Your body is perfect.
You don't ever have to disguise."

We all have growing up to do.
None of us are exempt
from smashing patriarchal norms
or from holding others in contempt.

So when I see a girl
with razor bumps like mine,
I'll give her a smile and a nod.
Let her know she's doing just fine.

ANATOMICAL ANOMALY

I'm stretched out on the operating table
like a splayed starfish underneath
a microscope.
The white light hurts my eyes.
There is liquid between my toes,
a brownish-grey substance I stepped on while
stripping into my surgical gown.
The center's a dump.
It smells like death and knock-off Clorox
but it's free so who am I to complain.
The doctor spreads my legs wide
and shoves his instrument inside
and I didn't even have a warning and
before I knew it,
I'm screaming
at the top of my
lungs.
He purposely didn't give me the anesthesia
like he was supposed to.
He quietly chuckles.
He says that's just his sudden reaction
to my yelling, but I know it's just
male pleasure
deriving
from female
pain.

I've been here before.

I'm sick of feeling like I have to piss
every two minutes.
I'm sick of pushing all my physical limits.
I'm tired of new doctors, new diagnoses, new clinics.
I'm tired of feeling like a freak,
a fraud,
a fucking gimmick.
The camera is yanked out of my urethra as I try not to seethe.
"Be happy you don't have cancer. You can now leave."
Tears fall down my cheeks as I wipe
the blood from my thighs.
I changed. He did not leave.
I still don't know what's wrong with me
after this failure of a cystoscopy.

I have seen more doctors this year
than I have seen friends.
More white walls,
cups full of urine
needles and ambulances
than I have seen
plays, gone to bars
or gotten drunk at parties.
The space that connects my
humerus to my elbow
has become raw
from IVs and blood
samples.
One time
they did both simultaneously
and I didn't even flinch
because I was so used to
getting stabbed.

"Your urethra is just tiny."
This M.D. reassured me.
Twelve urinary tract infections followed
and I have no more energy
because when they teach you about sex,
they don't tell you that you can get fucked
by your own anatomy.

LA SAGRADA FAMÍLIA

I wandered through the castle
as gold ricocheted
off the gigantic ivory pillars
and onto my ivory body.
A kaleidoscope wonderland
with such sacrality,
such perfection.
Each corner I rounded
was new.
Different hues and geometric
shapes shifted around me while
colossal paradigms shifted inside.
Where is my place in this world?

I didn't want to breathe
in fear of being too loud.
This is a place where
the only sound that should echo
through the chambers,
are your tear drops
smacking against the tile
as you take in the
otherworldly craftsmanship.

This place made me believe in God.
But that went away the moment
I left, meandering the seductive
and unforgiving streets
of Barcelona.

I recently craned my neck
and I remembered marveling at that
magnificence above me like I did
a few years ago.

It was last night
when you woke me
after falling asleep on your chest.
"Time to brush your teeth love."

I looked up at you
and for one brief moment,
I felt religion again.

I FORGOT MY PARACHUTE THIS TIME

It's a long way down from here. I pray I stick the landing
'cause my mistakes from this life are stuck to me like a branding.
Tiny, violent reminders of the women I used to be
are embedded in the skin and bones I no longer see,
for I've lost touch with every past version of me.

But the woman I am now is standing on the edge.
18,000 ft. higher and fully fledged.
My past safety nets woven with ego, shame and pride
are released from my grasp, I've got nothing to hide
now that I know who I am on the inside.

I'm leaning out of the Boeing and I see emerald plains below.
To my left is the Pacific and to the right, mountains of snow.
I'm going to free fall into this love, I know I'm ready to go.
This is the realest thing I have, and ever will know.

WOODS COVE

I remember being on the shore
when I was ten.
It was my first time seeing the ocean.
I sported a hot pink one-piece
with lavender butterflies
caressing my belly.
I felt ready.
I dipped my toes in
but ran away quickly from the cold.
The water was deceiving.
My little brother,
free of all inhibitions,
took my hand
and we went out to sea together. The ice water
numbed our bodies and we laughed and laughed
until the current swept us out too far
and there was no sand to stand on anymore.
He didn't know what to do to survive so he
submerged me underneath to stand upon my shoulders.
I lost all my breath.
I remember opening my panicked eyes
wondering if this was the last image I'd ever see on earth.
A blur of salt, blue and beige.
A Monet painting.
Luckily it wasn't.
The lifeguard dragged me out on a bright yellow buoy
and my mother hovered endless tears over me.
I didn't swim in the ocean for thirteen years after that.

When we were out in that water today, colliding into what felt like
brick walls, I thought back to when I was that little girl
and I remembered something.
I never had a fear of drowning.
I had a fear of not being saved.

I watched you return to the shoreline,
my back against the current.
Our eyes locked one last time
and I let the waves
swallow me whole.

LOVELORN

Her stare met mine across the bar
and I knew I could love her.
The way her hair fell,
how her teeth sharpened,
the way her hips stirred.
How those eyes felt like daggers to the chest
you couldn't look away from.
But she spread kindness like glitter
'cause she knew everyone could use some.
Knew she'd been bruised before
from those who tried to shape her to their mold.
But the calcium in her bones hardened,
a resilient spirit, cardiac muscle of gold.

I knew I could love her.
But she would not let me.
This woman was far too stubborn,
far too proud
and far too messy.
Her gaze left the glass
and it all became clearer.

I'll always be lovelorn with that
woman in the mirror.

Bonus Poems

THE ARSONIST

I wasn't supposed to make it.
The contractions came five months early
and I was screaming with everything
in my half-born of a body
hoping I would stay
safe inside.
Leaving my mother's womb
this soon
meant never coming back,
never being alive.
I held on for dear life.
Her screams echo in
the hospital room
and the catalyst of them was
one of impending doom.
My father was set ablaze
from the scrapping of metal
in a junkyard and
the sparks bounced off
his drill
much too quickly.
Flame swallowed him whole.

That was it.
The man I had not yet known,
but wanted to know,
had his skin
melting onto the floor
the parts of him left,
only bone.
My ma got the call
when she was alone
and she thought
it was over.
I was over —
we, were over.

But my father did not die.
My mother did not die
and I did not die.
Somehow
we all survived
this fire,

until the memories came flooding.
I didn't know what to do.
As my mind started to form,
I remembered burn victims
needed to treat their wounds too.
Cautiously,
meticulously.
They will go to
great lengths
to find relief,
even if it means burning you
to the ground in the process.

DOMESTIC LIFE

Our cat comes to the edge of the bathtub to kiss my face.
The remnants of her salmon feast
linger on my cheek
and you sit across from me
on the toilet seat
and put a joint between my fingers
as I soak.
You tell me how sexy I was in that play back in college,
but I feel even sexier now submerged in bubbles.
I don't need the blue glitter or the fishnets
or the black leather choker or the strobe lights.
We can talk like strangers for a little tonight.

You say you like my optimism best
and that the world would be better if there
were more people like me.
But I'm only thinking of how much
better the world would be if
there were more people like you,
full of rage, leaving no residue
if people upset you.
You're so honest.
You don't know what else to do.
That makes me humbled and want
to come through.

The bathwater is tepid now.
Hope my fever has sweated out.
All that's left of me is a silhouette now
because my warm body's in the bedroom somehow,
starving for your flesh.

I always wonder how
you get me here so quickly.

CHESS

Golden eyes loom over
my rooks and knights.
Sorry if I pick some fights
'cause I am black
and you're always white,
but my loss is the same
the colors don't mind.
Your intellect cuts like
our kitchen knives.
I hate this game so much,
I wish I had nine lives.
Let me win just once,
I promise it's not a crime.
My arms are tired
from the height of this climb.
You are superior at this,
it's already implied.
You can have everything on the table,
but let the queen survive.

MOTHER'S DAY

Mother, can you hear me
in agony, peace or rage?
You've taught me how to live,
a bird free from its cage.
You have made me headstrong,
you have made me kind,
you have made me patient,
you have made me wise.

Mother, can you hear me
in wisdom, pain or doubt?
A reminder from your daughter
who sometimes screams, sometimes shouts.
She may not be perfect,
she may not have much to give,
she may not be where she wants to be,
but she knows what it means to live.

Mother, can you hear me
in courage, love or fear?
I promise to always come running,
no matter how far or near.
I would run through all the canyons,
I would run through all the trees,
I would run through fields of flowers,
I would build a boat and brave open seas.

Mother, can you hear me.
In this poem for you I write.
I hope it brings you comfort
morning, noon or night.
For I love you so dearly
and I am lucky to be home.
All accolades go to you
when I see how well I've grown.

About the Author

Jordan Broberg is a recent graduate of USC's School of Dramatic Arts where she received her B.A. in Dramatic Arts with an Acting Emphasis. She is also a director and playwright. This is her first book.

Broberg was born in Glendora, California and currently resides in Los Angeles.

www.jordanbroberg.com

Photography by Tandem Photo

CPSIA information can be obtained
at www.ICGtesting.com
Printed in the USA
LVHW010431280421
685800LV00025B/643/J

9 781662 911576